My First Dharma Book

By Christine H. Huynh, M.D.

Illustrations by RKS Illustrations

Front Cover by Thu Ann Dao

2nd Edition

Dharma Wisdom, LLC

My First Dharma Book

Bringing the Buddha's Teachings into Practice series

Copyright © 2021 by Dharma Wisdom, LLC

All rights reserved.

Published in the United States of America by Dharma Wisdom, LLC. No part of this book may be reproduced or transmitted in any form or by any means, electronic or mechanical, including photocopying, recording, or by any information storage and retrieval system without the prior written permission of the author, except for the inclusion of brief quotations in critical reviews and certain other noncommercial uses permitted by copyright law. For permission requests or information, please contact the publisher.

Dharma Wisdom, LLC
Arlington, Texas
www.DharmaWisdomDW.com
books@DharmaWisdomDW.com

Author: Christine H. Huynh, M.D.
Front Cover Illustrator:
Thu Ann Dao
Back Cover and Interior
Illustrator: RKS Illustrations

Library of Congress
Control Number: 2021910170

ISBN: 978-1-951175-15-3

Second Edition 2021

Dharma is the teaching of the truth.
It is the Buddha's teaching that
shows understanding and love.

The Dharma shows me the Way and teaches me how to live my best life now.

It says that I have the
Buddha-nature in me.

My Buddha-nature tells me:

1) Do not do what is bad.

2) Do what is good.

3) Keep my mind pure and calm.

This is what the Buddha teaches.

My Buddha-nature is always present in me.
It is my awakened mind and natural goodness.

It shines deep within just as bright as the sun.

My Buddha-nature can become
dull with wrongdoings, just like
a mirror covered with dust.

I keep my mind clean and clear
for it to always shine bright.

By avoiding
the 5 wrongdoings:

1) I will not
harm living
creatures
just for
fun.

2) I will not
take what
is not mine.

3) I will not
leave a
good friend
in need.

4) I will not tell lies to hurt others, or say unkind words. I will be patient to listen and not quick to judge.

YOU ARE UGLY

5) I will not eat too much of the food that is bad for me, as it will harm my mind and body.

And I should avoid unhealthy games and entertainment, which can impair mindful thinking.

There are 5 right things I will do:

1) I will protect and care for the critters on this earth, whether big or small.

2) I will share with others the things that have been given to me.

3) I will keep long lasting friendships.

4) I will speak the truth with only loving speech to earn my trust. And listen deeply to understand.

5) I will choose healthy food, as well as pleasant games and shows, to nourish my mind and body.

There are 5 things I should
not do. And there are 5 things
I will always try to do.
This training protects me
from having problems in life.

5 CEPTS

These 5 rules are the very basic for me to live by. They are called precepts, the teachings of morality. This practice benefits me and others.

Precepts help to prevent simple faults and halt any misdeeds.

Precepts help me to always do the right thing, through my thoughts, speech, and actions.

When I do good things, everyone is happy.
When I do bad things, everyone is unhappy.

DHARMA LIFE

So now I have read and learned about my Buddha-nature and the Five Precepts.

SHARING
IS
CARING

START

FOLLOW
THE
5 PRECEPTS

DEEP
LISTENING
LOVING
SPEECH
SPEAK
TRUTHFULLY

I must put them
into practice
and apply them
to my daily life.

PLEASE   SORRY   THANK YOU

FINISH

MY
AWAKENED
MIND

EAT
FRUITS
AND
VEGGIES

Let's review the 5 wrongdoings and the 5 right things I will do, to tune my thoughts, speech, and actions with examples too.

DON'Ts:

1. HARMING
2. STEALING
3. BETRAYING
4. LYING
5. NON- NOURISHING

DOs:

1. CARING
2. SHARING
3. BEFRIENDING
4. LISTENING
5. NOURISHING

1) How can I be caring and protect the living critters on this earth? I think of the safety for the mother deer so she can nurture her fawn. I plead my friends not to aim rocks and arrows at her. And this is how I prevent harming creatures just for fun.

2) How can I share with others the blessings I have received? I think of all the wonderful books that have been given to me. I exchange the books with my friends to share. This prevents any mishap of taking what is not mine.

3) How can I remain faithful in my friendship? I think of the special times of hide and seek that my friends and I played together. When my friend falls with an injury, I will not leave a friend in need. And I vow not to forsake one another when new friends come along.

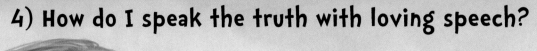

4) How do I speak the truth with loving speech?

I think of the outcome of telling white lies. One lie leads to another, it will multiply. I tell my mom with honesty that I did not do my chores. So she can trust me forevermore.

5) How can I choose healthy food to nourish my mind and body? I think of the fresh fruits and vegetables that come from the earth and sun. The sweets and fried food should be avoided, as they can cloud my thinking. I must not forget to choose the pleasant games and shows, and avoid the unwholesome ones.

I will follow these precepts to keep my mind shining bright.

And have my Buddha-nature
glow like a starry night.

May this teaching be planted
in everyone's mind.

As the Dharma teachings will
be present beyond all lifetime.

I must remember to practice for my Buddha-nature to always shine within me.

Made in the USA
Monee, IL
11 September 2021

77811789R00021